DOCKSIDE

STAGE **3**

BOOK 7

DARK CASTLE

Philippa Bateman

RISING★STARS

It was pizza and DVD night.

"What's the DVD, Dad?" asked JJ.

"It's *Dark Castle*," said Dad.

"Ok. Let's sit apart!" said Tasha.

Dad pressed start on the DVD player.
After a while ...

This part is so bad!
I can't look!

Just then the flat went dark.
They all gasped!

"It's a power cut. Let me get a torch," said Dad. "I'll come too," said JJ.

"You are a wimp," said Tasha.

Tasha and mum waited in the dark.

"Let's have a laugh," said Tasha.
"When they come back, let's freak
them out!"

They hid behind the arm of the sofa.

When Dad and JJ came back in ...